ECLIPSE MIRACLE

The Sun is the Same Size as The Moon in The Sky

WRITTEN & ILLUSTRATED BY SAND SHEFF

Hole in the Rock Publishing
Moab, Utah

Thank you to my family and friends
for your encouragement and support.
Thank you to Tamara Dever at TLC Graphics
for doing such a wonderful design.
Thank you to Sunnie. Thanks to God.
For Nick and Ivy.

Eclipse Miracle: The Sun's The Same Size as The Moon in The Sky
© 2017 Sand Sheff. All rights reserved.

Published by Hole in the Rock Publishing, Moab, Utah

Illustrations by Sand Sheff

Cover and interior design by TLC Graphics, www.TLCGraphics.com

Softcover: ISBN 978-0-9988445-0-3
Hardcover: ISBN 978-0-9988445-1-0

When I consider thy heavens, the work of thy fingers,

the moon and the stars, which thou hast ordained;

What is man, that thou art mindful of him?

and the son of man, that thou visitest him?

PSALM 8: 3-4

The Sun is the same size...

As the Moon in the sky.

It's hard to tell

since we don't

see them stand side by side.

Besides, the sun is just

way too bright for our eyes,

So why do I say,

"THE SUN AND MOON

LOOK JUST THE SAME SIZE"?

Well, once a dark cloud passed over the sun. The Sun's shape shone through for a second, then it was gone. It looked almost like a full Moon at night, when it's high in the sky and shining its light.

I turned away fast from that cloud in the sky.
We never look at the sun — it hurts people's eyes!
But I couldn't stop wondering if it's possibly true;

DOES THE SUN APPEAR
JUST THE SAME SIZE AS THE MOON?

So I hopped on a comet

because I thought it would be fun

TO FIND OUT A SECRET

ABOUT THE MOON

AND THE SUN.

The Sun is a great ball of fire.
And it's quite far away.

Our Moon is
dusty and small;
Close to Earth
is where it stays.

But God
made them both
and placed them
just right;

So that
one rules
the day
and one rules
the night.

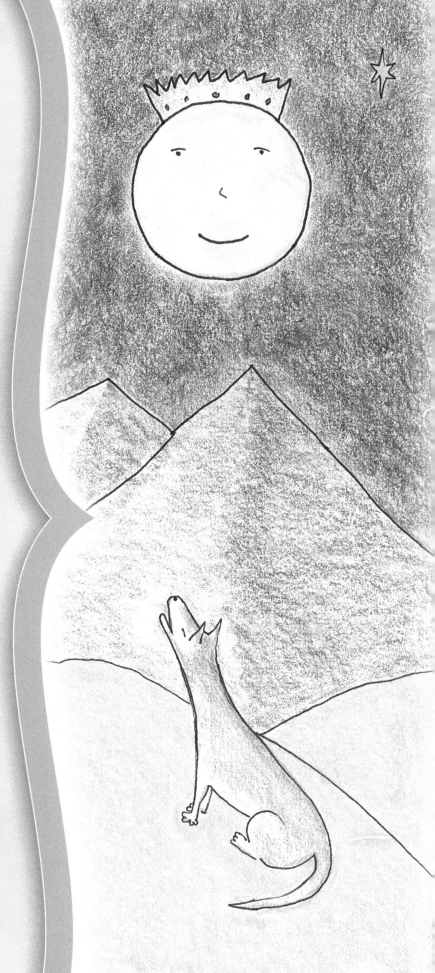

The Sun is 400 times
bigger than the Moon,
so they say.

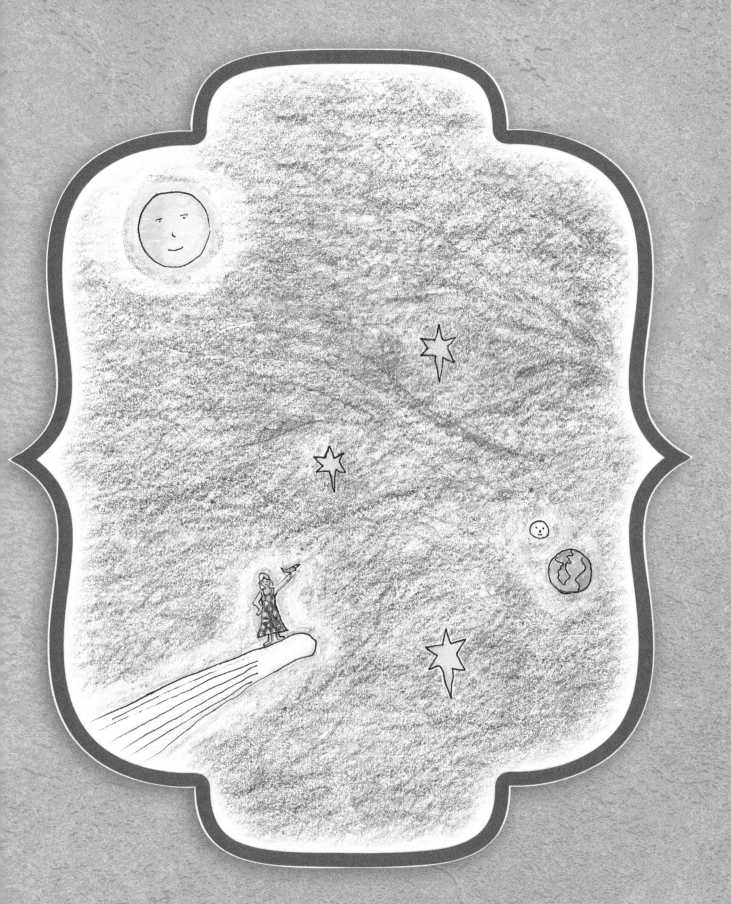

But it's also 400 times further away.

So though Sun's huge and far;
and Moon's small and near,

THAT'S BECAUSE DISTANCE CHANGES
THE WAY THAT WE SEE;

Just hold your thumb out

and you can make it as big as a tree!

Or if you're at home,

close one eye and

pull back your thumb.

You might be able to

make it as tall as your Mom.

The Sun helps plants grow.

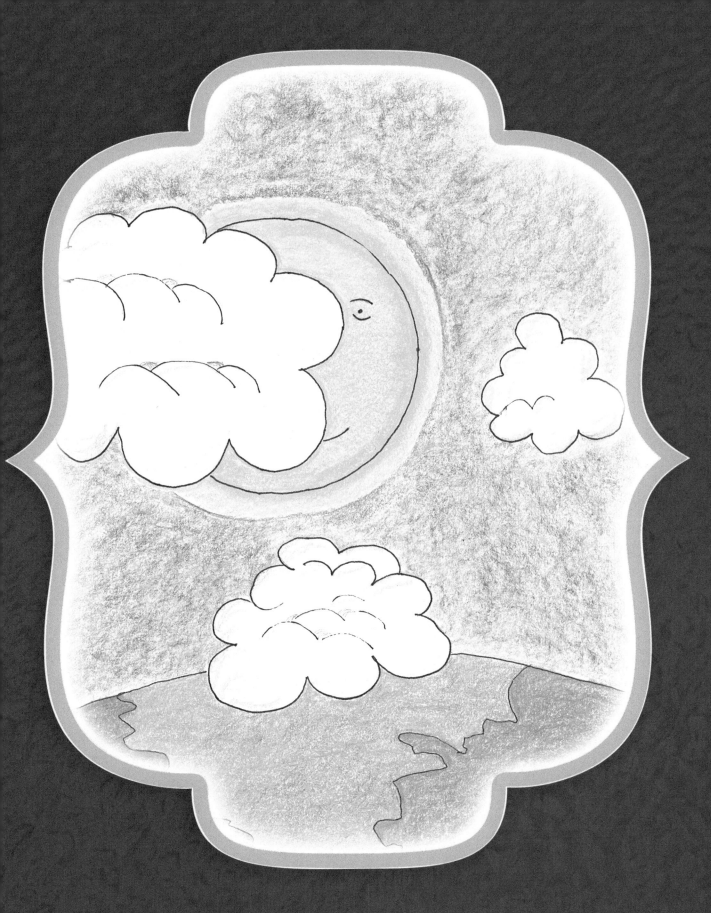

And makes puffy clouds form.

23

It comes up every morning to keep the animals warm.

The Moon rises too, but looks different each day;
From new up to full, and then back the same way.

The
new Moon
is dark;
it hides
in the
night.

but it
comes back
a crescent;
a thin,
pretty light.

OUR MOONLIGHT IS BRIGHTER THAN ON NEIGHBOR PLANETS:
and though sometimes we may
take this blessing for granted;
We know it makes the night friendly
to have that soft light.
Earth is special to see such
bright moonlight at night.

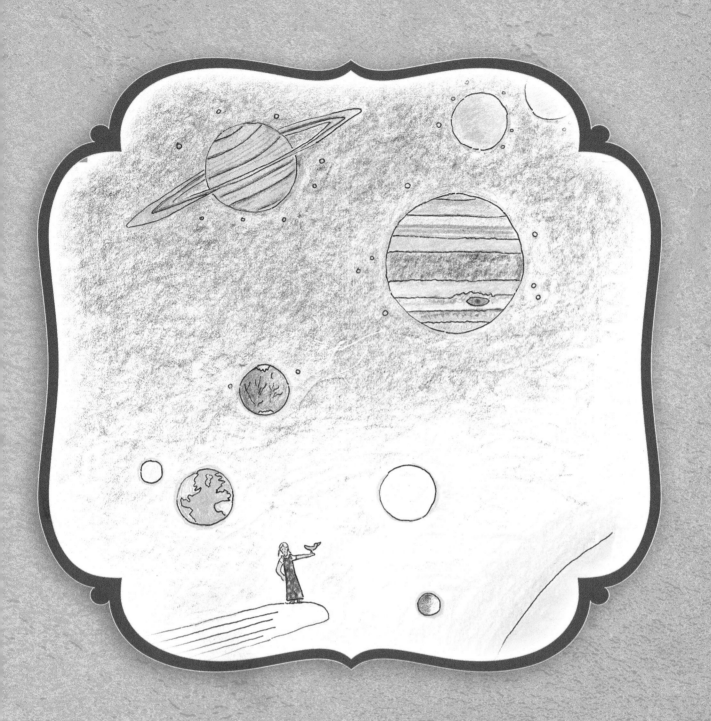

In our whole solar system,
from Mercury to Neptune
No place else sees
a same-sized Sun and Moon.

And of course, Earth is also the only place
that we know where there are animals...

And trees...

And children who grow.

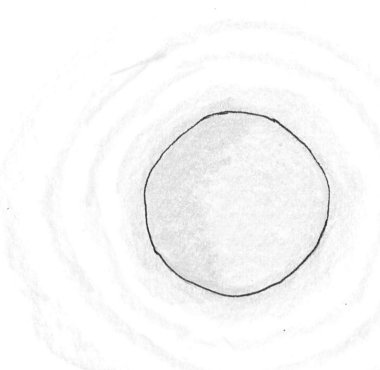

WE DON'T LOOK AT THE SUN;
it can blind people's eyes;
And we don't ever see
Sun and Moon side by side –
So how could we know
they appear in the sky
the same size?

BECAUSE OF AN EVENT VERY RARE

CALLED A SOLAR ECLIPSE;

When the Moon goes

in front of the Sun for a bit.

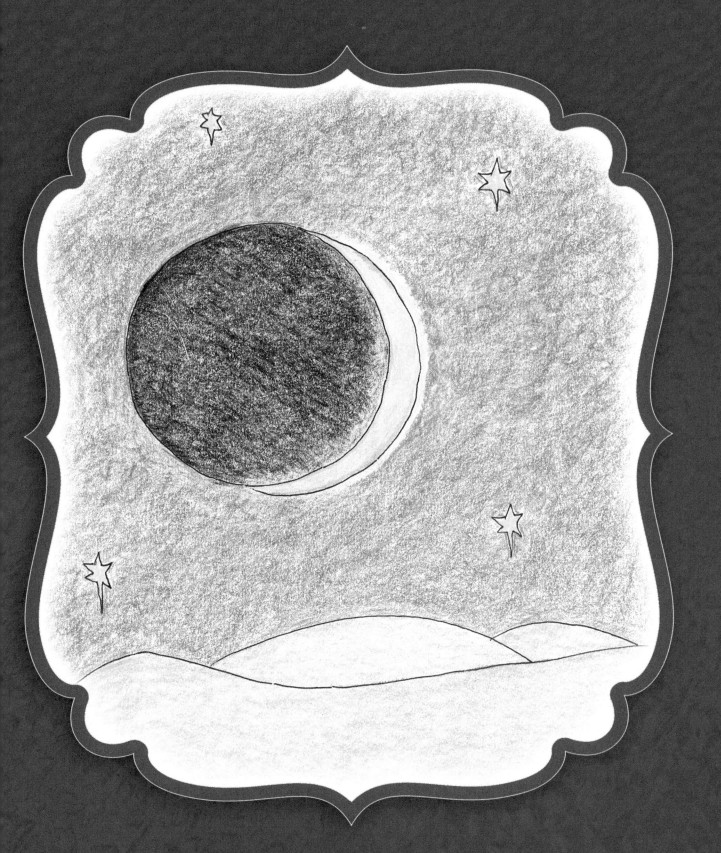

Until they perfectly match up exactly in line;
And it gets dark in the day and the stars start to shine.

Finally,
the only thing left
of that fiery old Sun,
Is its blue-white corona—
the only time we
ever see one.

And as for the animals,
they hardly know what to do.
Because now it's dark in the day,
and the sky isn't blue.

But then the Moon it moves on and daylight returns.
The Sun was not gone for long —
but a lesson was learned.

Because the people who saw begin to realize
That from Earth, Sun and Moon look like
they're just the same size!

I KNOW IT CAN'T BE JUST CHANCE

we get to see such a dance

between those beautiful heavenly balls;

They shine with a light

which by day and by night

Brightens the way for us all.

I'm so thankful our planet was given this view
Of the sun and the moon and the stars;
We've been perfectly placed in a great outer space
To remind us how special we are.

A message was written
in the heavens above:
God made this Earth and He made it with love.

44

COMMON KNOWLEDGE
SUN AND MOON
Facts & Observations

A Key to the Text

The Sun's the same size as the Moon in the Sky.

Well, they are basically the same size. But they vary ever so slightly depending on orbits. From Earth, the angular diameter (apparent size) of the Moon and the Sun are both 0.5 degrees or approximately 30 arc minutes. The orbits of the Moon around the Earth and the Earth around the Sun are both elliptical, so the angular diameter can vary slightly. Still, the similarity in apparent diameters remains very close. Sun and Moon average 98% similarity in apparent size. That would be the difference between viewing a person who was 5 foot 6 inches, 150 pounds and a person who was five foot 5 inches and 147 pounds. Pretty close. There are times when the apparent sizes are essentially identical or the Moon appears slightly larger, which allows for the perfection of the solar eclipse phenomenon. Because the Moon's orbit is moving slightly away (3.8 cm or 1.5 inches a year), scientists tend to say that in the distant past, the Moon appeared much larger than the Sun. Likewise, in the distant future, the Moon will appear smaller. This is a unique time. Apparently, intelligent human viewers appeared on Earth during a special time when the Sun/Moon sky diameter is identical.

It's hard to tell since we don't ever see Sun and Moon side by side. Besides, the sun's just way too bright for our eyes.

The moon is often visible in the daytime sky, but becomes invisible the closer it appears to the sun-which it does around the new moon. When full, the Moon is exactly opposite the Sun. This means that the Moon rises just as the Sun is setting, and sets just as the Sun is rising. The full Moon is also the only night in the month when a lunar eclipse can happen. A lunar eclipse is when the Earth's shadow goes across the Moon. This is a very different

45

phenomenon than a solar eclipse. Total lunar eclipses happen on Earth on average about one full Moon out of six and some years there are none.

The best times in the month to see the Moon in daylight are close to first and last quarter (what some call a half moon), when the Moon is 90 degrees away from the Sun in the sky.

But once a dark cloud passed over the Sun; The Sun's shape shone through for a second, then it was gone. I thought it had almost looked like a full Moon at night—When it's high in the sky, shining its light. Then I turned away fast from that cloud in the sky. We never look at the sun; it hurts people's eyes! But I couldn't stop wondering if it was possibly true; does the Sun really appear the same size as the Moon?

You cannot safely view the Sun directly without special equipment. Certain unique dark clouds with just the right thickness can occasionally allow someone to glance up and briefly consider the apparent size of the Sun without the usual overwhelming and dangerous glare. Such glimpses are always momentary. Any effort to directly view the Sun (except when it is in total eclipse) will hurt your eyes. Permanent blindness can occur from staring at the sun. **Never, Ever, Ever, look at the sun through a telescope or binoculars, not even for a second!** Magnifying lenses concentrate the sun's rays, causing immediate damage. The sun can only be viewed directly when special filters (such as a welding mask) are properly deployed.

The best and safest way to view the Sun is indirectly, by building a small pinhole projector. Anyone can do this in three easy steps.

1) Take Two Pieces of Cardboard or cardstock each the size of a dinner plate. Paper works but it tends to be too floppy to handle easily.

2) Poke a pin sized hole through the center of one as cleanly as possible.

3) With your back to the sun, hold the cardboard with the hole in it closest to the sun and, holding the other piece at arm's length; project the image onto the other piece of cardboard. When done correctly, this simple method projects a perfect and totally safe image of the sun.

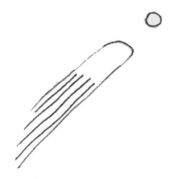

So I hopped on this comet; because I thought it'd be fun, to find out a secret about the Moon and the Sun.

A comet is a small, icy object that orbits the Sun and has a long "tail" of gas. They can take thousands of years to orbit the sun; Comets are made of ice, dust, and tiny pieces of rock. Sometimes they are visible to people on Earth. When the Earth's orbit takes it through a comets' tail, the dust burns up in our atmosphere and results in a meteor shower.

The Sun's diameter is 864,938 miles across (1.392 million km). You could line up 109  Earths across its face. The Sun has a circumference of 2,713,406 miles across (4.37 million km). You could fit 1.3 million Earths inside the Sun. You could fit 64.3 million Moons inside the Sun. The Sun contains 99.8 % of the mass of the entire solar system. The "fire" created by the Sun's core is apparently nuclear fusion. Temperatures inside the Sun can reach 27 million degrees Fahrenheit (15 million degrees Celsius).

Despite being almost 865 thousand miles across, there is only a 6 mile difference in the Sun's polar and equatorial diameters. It is the closest thing to a perfect sphere yet observed in nature.

It takes eight minutes for light to reach Earth from the Sun. The speed of light is 186,000 miles per second.

The Sun rotates in the opposite direction to Earth with the Sun rotating from west to east instead of east to west like Earth.

The temperature on the Moon can vary between 250 degrees to -350 degrees Fahrenheit — a 600 degree variance, depending on whether you are in sunlight or shadow. The Moon has no air of any kind.

Only one face of the Moon is ever seen from Earth. This is because the Moon rotates on its axis at exactly the same rate it takes to orbit Earth. This phenomenon is known as "tidal locking". The side we see from Earth is illuminated by sunlight, while the "dark" side has only been seen by the human eye from spacecraft. The rise and fall of tides on Earth is caused by the Moon. Two bulges exist due to the gravitational pull the Moon exerts. One is on the side facing the Moon and the other on the side facing away from it. These bulges move around the oceans as the Earth rotates which causes the high and low tides found across the globe.

You weigh much less on the Moon. Due to its small mass, the Moon has much weaker gravity than Earth. You would weigh one sixth (about 16.5%) of your Earth weight while on the Moon.

No sound can be heard on the Moon and the sky is always black.

The Moon is the fifth largest natural satellite in the solar system. Still, its diameter (2,159 miles) is about the distance from Chicago to Los Angeles.

But God made them both and placed them
just right, So that one rules the day
and one rules the night.

And God said, Let there be lights in the firmament of the heaven to divide the day from the night; and let them be for signs, and for seasons, and for days, and years: And let them be for lights in the firmament of the heaven to give light upon the earth: and it was so. And God made two great lights; the greater light to rule the day, and the lesser light to rule the night: he made the stars also. And God set them in the firmament of the heaven

to give light upon the earth, to rule over the day and over the night, and to divide the light from the darkness: and God saw that it was good.
Genesis 1:14-18 (KJV)

This Creation account is found in the Hebrew Torah, (or the first five books of the Bible). which comprise some of the oldest writings still widely read in the world.

Sun's four hundred times bigger than Moon, so they say; but it's also 400 times further away.

This statement is accepted and often repeated as a true representation by astronomers. The Sun has a diameter 400.5 times larger than the Moon. Obviously, this figure stays consistent.

The Sun, on average, is a distance of around 93 million miles from Earth. But the actual distance can vary between 91.5 million miles (147 million km) and about 94.5 million miles (152 million km). Earth's orbit is not a perfect circle. It is shaped more like an oval, or ellipse. Over the course of a year, Earth moves sometimes close to the Sun (becoming closest being around Jan. 3rd) and sometimes farther away (the farthest around July 4th). The Moon also has an elliptical orbit and its distance from Earth varies between 225 and 252 thousand miles. On average, the moon is 238,000 miles away.

The average is rarely the reality. For one instance, when the Sun is 92,000,000 miles away and the Moon is 230,000, the Moon is exactly 400 times closer than Sun.

So though Sun's huge and far; and Moon's small and near, in the sky, the same size is how they appear.

That's because distance changes the way that we see; just hold your thumb out; you can make it as big as a tree! Or if you're at home, close one eye and pull back your thumb. You might be able to make it as tall as your Mom.

You can experiment with perspective yourself. Take a basketball or other large ball and set it down or have someone hold it. Then take a marble with you and find the place where the marble perfectly covers the basketball. That will be the place where the exact difference in the sizes of the ball and marble are matched by the difference in distance.

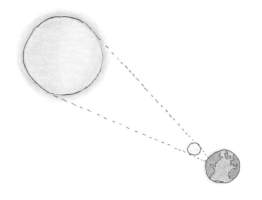

The Sun helps plants grow; And makes puffy clouds form. It comes up every morning to keep the animals warm.

All plants need sunlight to make their food in a process that is called photosynthesis. Where there is no ultraviolet light at all, there can be no living plants.

Clouds are formed when the sun warms water. Moist, warm air rises and expands in the atmosphere. Rising water vapor condenses into water droplets which make up clouds. When the vapor cools, rain falls.

Sunlight is vital for all animals to survive. The Earth's relatively warm climate allows for life. Even those animals that live in dark, cold places rely on the food that has been produced through the Sun's warmth. For instance, bats need bugs that need sunlight and aquatic animals at the bottom of the ocean need decayed matter that falls from near the surface to initiate the food chain.

The Moon rises too, but looks different
each day; from new up to full,
and then back the same way.
The new Moon's so dark, it hides
in the night. But it comes back
a crescent: a soft, pretty light.

When Sun and Moon are aligned on the same side of the Earth, the Moon is "new", and the side of the Moon facing Earth is not illuminated by the Sun. As the Moon *waxes*, the amount of lit surface as seen from Earth is increasing. The lunar phase's progress through new moon, crescent moon, first-quarter moon (sometimes commonly called "half-moon", gibbous moon, and full moon. The moon is then said to *wane* as it passes through the gibbous moon, third-quarter moon, and crescent moon and back to new moon. During a crescent Moon, the phenomenon of earthshine may be apparent, where the night side of the Moon faintly reflects light from Earth.

Our moonlight is brighter than on our
neighbor planets; and though sometimes
we may take this blessing for granted;
we know it makes the night friendlier
to have a good light. Earth is special to
have such bright moonlight at night.

Moonlight is, of course, just reflected sunlight. Due to the Moon's large size and Earth's relatively clear atmosphere, no other planet in the solar system receives anything close to the amount of moonlight that Earth does. This is true even though the full Moon's light is about 1,000,000 times fainter than the Sun.

In our whole solar system,
from Mercury to Neptune; No place else
sees a same-sized Sun and a Moon.

Scientists agree that Earth's sun/moon arrangement is unique in our solar system. There is no scientific "reason" for this arrangement, and it is usually referred to by scientists as a coincidence—or even the "great coincidence".

Mercury and Venus, the innermost planets, have no moons. Earth has one Moon; the largest moon of any rocky planet in the Solar System. Mars has two moons, Phobos and Deimos. Both are small odd-shaped rocks. The biggest is less than 15 miles across.

Jupiter has 67 known moons. Jupiter possesses the largest moon in the solar system, Ganymede, which is more than a thousand miles wider than our moon. Its eight larger moons are called Galilean moons, since they were discovered by Galileo, the inventor of the telescope. Jupiter itself is huge, 88,000 miles across and two and a half times the mass of all the other planets and moons combined. It is a gassy planet with no known surface.

Saturn has 62 moons with confirmed orbits; seven moons are large, including Titan, the second largest moon in the Solar System. The rings of Saturn are made up of icy objects ranging in size from less than an inch to hundreds of feet across, each of which is on its own orbit about the planet. Saturn is also a gassy planet with no known surface.

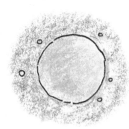

Uranus has 27 named moons, five of which are big while Neptune has 14 moons, the largest of which is called Triton. Uranus and Neptune are gassy planets,

The dwarf planet Pluto has five moons. Its largest moon is called Charon, It is about half as large (about 750 miles across) as Pluto itself, and large enough to orbit a point outside Pluto's surface.

Earth is the only place
that we know
Where there are animals...
Trees....
and children who grow.

Earth is the only known planet on which life exists. All other planets in our solar system are covered with lifeless soil or poisonous gases.

Some type of life is found in every niche on the Earth, from frozen Antarctica to the baking Saharan desert. From the top of the atmosphere to the bottom of the oceans,

and even underground, life finds a home on our planet. To this day no sign of any kind of life has been found on another planet. There are many special qualities of Earth's situation that allow for life to flourish here. One of them is our distance from the Sun. If we were any farther away, our planet would be too cold. Any closer and it would be too hot. Scientists often refer to our position in space as the "Goldilocks'" zone. It's just right!

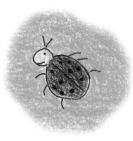

If Earth rotated on its axis slower, life would soon die, either by freezing at night because of lack of heat from the sun, or by burning during the day from too much sun.

If the Moon were much closer to us, huge tides would overflow onto the lowlands. If it were much further away, we would not have significant tides, which help cleanse both ocean and land.

The Earth is the only planet known to have large bodies of water—70% of the earth's surface area consists of oceans, lakes, and seas. Water also acts as a stabilizer for Earth's temperature and provides the chemical foundation of all life.

The Sun is a special kind of star: warm, medium-sized and stable. Most stars in the universe are dwarfs or giants.

The mixture of gases in our atmosphere is perfect for life. If it were much different (more oxygen or nitrogen, less carbon dioxide, etc., or the atmospheric pressure was much lighter or heavier), life would cease to exist on Earth.

If our atmosphere were thinner, meteors would be constantly pounding the Earth's surface. Instead, most typically burn up high above us, providing us with the beautiful phenomenon of shooting stars.

The chances of a planet being just the right size, with water, the right distance away from the right star, with the right gases and the right sized moon etc., must be extremely tiny. The mathematical odds (if they could even be calculated) are certainly billions to one!

> We don't look at the Sun;
> it can blind people's eyes;
> And we don't ever see Sun and Moon
> side by side. So how could we know
> they appear in the sky
> the same size?
> Because of an event very rare event
> called a solar eclipse;
> When the Moon goes in front
> of the Sun for a bit.

An eclipse of the Sun can only occur at New Moon when the Moon passes between Earth and Sun. Literally; the Moon goes in front of the Sun.

The track of the Moon's shadow is called the Path of Totality. It is typically around 10,000 miles long but less than 100 miles wide. In order to see the Sun become completely eclipsed by the Moon, you must be somewhere inside that narrow path of totality. Just one total eclipse occurs on average somewhere on earth every 18 months. Since each total eclipse is only visible from a very narrow ribbon of the earth's surface, it is rare to see one. You'd have to wait an average of more than 350 years between eclipses from any one place on Earth. Most people live their whole lives without ever seeing a total solar eclipse. The total phase of a solar eclipse rarely lasts more than a few minutes. It is considered to be one of the most breathtaking sights in all of nature. Not every eclipse of the Sun is a total eclipse. Sometimes, due to its orbit, the Moon appears too small to cover the entire Sun. The result of this arrangement is called an annular eclipse, sometimes referred to as a "Ring of Fire" eclipse.

Below are all of the total solar eclipses in a ten-year period starting in 2015. There are just seven in all. This shows the rarity of a true total solar eclipse.

- March 20, 2015: North Pole and the North Atlantic

- March 9, 2016: Indonesia and Micronesia

- August 21, 2017: west to east across the USA

- July 2, 2019: Argentina and Chile

- December 14, 2020: Polynesia, Argentina, and Chile

- December 4, 2021: Antarctica

- April 8, 2024: Mexico, USA, and Canada

Until they perfectly match up exactly
in line it gets dark in the day
and the stars start to shine.
Finally the only thing left
of that fiery old Sun, Is its
blue-white corona — the only time
we'll ever see one. And as for
the animals, they hardly know
what to do, Because now it's dark
in the day, and the sky isn't blue.

Animals typically get very quiet, and some head back to roost, during the totality portion of a solar eclipse. Birds usually stop singing. Likewise, some nocturnal animals start to wake up, thinking that night has fallen.

But then the Moon it moves on and
daylight returns. The Sun was not gone
for long, but still a lesson was learned.

Because the people who saw begin
to realize From Earth, Sun and Moon
look just the same size! I know it can't
be just chance we get to see such a dance
between those beautiful heavenly balls;
they shine with a light which by day
and by night Brightens the way
for us all. I'm so thankful our planet
was given this view of the sun and
the moon and the stars; we've been
perfectly placed in a great outer space
to remind us how special we are.

It is our choice as to how we wish to view the indisputable arrangement of Sun and Moon in our skies. Many just say "coincidence" and are done with it. Others come to the conclusion that this is the intentional construction of a conscious Creator. Considering this idea is probably good for the brain and soul, regardless of one's final conclusions.

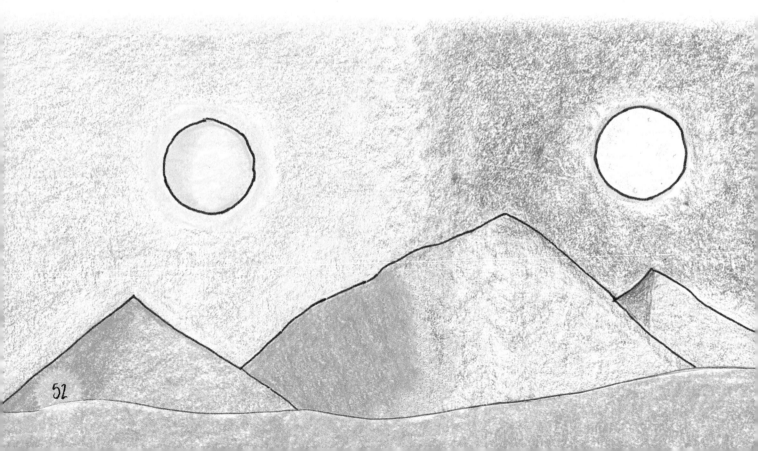

CPSIA information can be obtained
at www.ICGtesting.com
Printed in the USA
BVOW05s1714180817
492229BV00015B/73/P